Save A Life Today Ministries Inc.

SEASONED SALT

"Heirloom Edition"

Time Tested Principles Straight From
a Mother's Heart

Ida Hathman

SEASONED SALT

Copyright © 2019 by Ida Hathman.

All rights reserved.

No part of this book may be reproduced or transmitted in any form or by any means, electronic or mechanical, including photocopying, recording, or by any information storage and retrieval system, without permission in writing from the copyright author, except for the use of brief quotations in a book review.

ISBN: 978-1-970135-24-4 (Paperback)
978-1-970135-27-5 (Hardcover)

Published in the United States by Pen2Pad Ink Publishing.

Requests to publish work from this book or to contact the author should be sent to: ibhathman@att.net

Ida Hathman retains the rights to all images.

Interior design: Pen2Pad Ink Publishing

Table of Contents

The Transformation Begins
Foreword	6
Vision	9
Covenant to Love	11
S.A.L.T Foundational Scriptures	12

A Woman and Her Purpose
Understanding Your Purpose	14
Identifying Who You Are	20
Shaped for Serving God	26
We Were Formed for God's Family	32
Linking Your Purpose and Mission	41

A Woman and Her God
A Prayer That Changes Things	49
Devotion	67
Worshiping in Spirit and Truth	73
Woman's Formation	81
Growing in God	92

A Woman and Her Body
The Challenge to Change	106
Self-Esteem Matters	113
Understanding Who You Are	128

Message From The Author	132
Acknowledgements	133
About the Author	135

SEASONED SALT

The Transformation Begins

Foreword

As a psychotherapist who is Christian first, I must be sensitive to the spiritual concerns as well as the mental health deficits of my clients. But, there is a third branch of the balance tripod that also needs to be addressed. If your physical health is out of alignment, the other two areas will be more difficult to maintain.

Mother Ida Hathman nails the trifecta with this book! She suggests that if you do not consult God first, then no matter how hard you work for your mental and physical wellness, you will not be able to live your best life. When you meet Ida, you will know you have encountered one who has found her purpose in this life. Hopefully, you have already experienced love. But, just in case you haven't...get ready! Every time she sees me she grabs my face with both hands and kisses my cheeks about seventeen times! To know her is to love her and to know that she loves you genuinely. *This* is the love of God. If you are reading this right now you are about to understand this kind of love. You're about to be guided through finding your purpose in this love and in this life.

Ida makes two particular statements in this book that caught my attention. She says, "our most effective ministry will come out of our deepest hurt." I got concerned when I first read this because I thought maybe I wasn't operating effectively in my ministry, which is also my career as a therapist. I had to do a self-search to discover my deepest hurt because it's something I don't often think about it. I came up with the two people in my life that played the most negative roles in it, but positively shaped my ministry. I watched one take advantage of every single person in her life. I experienced the pain first hand from the other because it was me that was hurt. Neither of them considered how their actions affected those in their path. Only what they wanted mattered and each of them remain that way to this day.

As a therapist, I make sure to give my clients what I did not get from those two people. Counseling is all about the client. I cannot do my job effectively if I do not listen or allow God to work through me. I have to thank Ida for confirming that I am on the right track! She also states "...the greatest gift we can give someone is our time." My clients have an entire hour to themselves when they are with me and it is all about them! So, in reading this manuscript I have learned not only is my ministry effective, but I am also a great gift giver! By the end of this literary journey I was super excited. I'm still excited. Sure, there are things that I need to do in order to continue to grow personally, professionally and spiritually but I am walking in my purpose.

You *want* to read this book. You *need* to read this book. If at all possible, get in the presence of this amazing woman of God. You will not be disappointed. Let Ida give you the steps and walk with you through your endeavor to uncover your purpose. We each have a responsibility to do our parts in and for the Kingdom, but you have to do the work. To pull this off you need a support system and a family to make your work easier. There is no better time than now and no better facilitator than Mother Ida Hathman. It's your life and she wants you to live it on purpose!

Soneakqua J. White, M.A.,LPC
Licensed Professional Counselor
Author of *A Time to Heal* and *Red Flag!*

Vision

Changing, Enhancing and Seasoning Lives through the Word of God

Save A Life Today Ministries Inc. (S. A. L. T.) is a non-profit organization with a mission to equip the saints for the work of the ministry by ministering to the heart, mind and soul of God's woman (the total woman).

S. A. L. T. seeks to season the lives of women with an appropriate level of flavor according to Biblical and professional principles in three major ministry areas:

Psychological - To minister to the emotional, mental and behavioral needs of the woman.

Spiritual - To minister to the spiritual needs of the woman.

Physiological - To minister to the physical needs of the woman.

Save A Life Today's goal is to facilitate and equip women with an enlightened understanding of their true purpose in life, special gifts and unique roles. In doing so, the "total woman" will be equipped from the inside-out to do the work of the ministry.

"Salt is good, but if the salt loses its flavor, how will you season it? Have salt in yourselves, and have peace with one another." Mark 9:50

"You are the salt of the earth..." Matthew 5:13

In this book, you will embark on a journey towards truly discovering yourself and your purpose. Allow this book to be your guide as you learn your authentic identity and learn to love who were meant to be before the world dictated who you had to be.

Covenant to Love
I Corinthians 13

"Now I will show you the most excellent way.

If I speak in the tongues of men and of angels, but have not love, I am only a resounding gong or a clanging symbol.

If I have the gift of prophecy and can fathom all mysteries and all knowledge, and if I have faith that can move mountains, but have not love, I gain nothing.

If I give all I possess to the poor and surrender my body to the flames, but have not love, I gain nothing.

Love is patient, love is kind. It does not envy, it does not boast, it is not proud. It is not rude, it is not self-seeking, it is not easily angered, it keeps no record of wrongs. Love does not delight in evil, but rejoices with the truth. It always protects, always trusts, always hopes, always perseveres.

Love never fails. But where there are prophecies, they will cease; where there are tongues, they will be stilled; where there is knowledge, it will pass away. For we know in part and we prophecy in part, but when perfection comes, the imperfect disappears.

When I was a child, I talked like a child, I thought like a child, I reasoned like a child. When I became a man, I put childish ways behind me."

S.A.L.T.
Foundational Scriptures

Roman 12.1- 2 NKJV

I beseech you therefore brethren, by the mercies of God, that you present your bodies a living sacrifice, holy, acceptable unto God, which is your reasonable service. And do not be conformed to this world, but be transformed by the renewing of your mind, that you may prove what is that good, acceptable, and perfect, will of God.

II Corinthians 3:18 NKJV

But we all with unveiled face, beholding as in a mirror the glory of the Lord, are being transformed into the same image from glory to glory, just as by the spirit of the Lord.

A Woman and Her Purpose

Understanding Your Purpose

At one point or another many of us have found ourselves questioning our existence. Especially when nothing in life seems to be happening the way we need or desire for it to. In the book, *The Purpose Driven Life*, Author Rick Warren states your life isn't about you. It's about God. God specifically created you to fulfill a purpose that exceeds your own life-long hopes and dreams. You were created by His purpose and for His purpose. Thus, your existence is not an accident. Long before you were conceived in your mother's womb, you were conceived in the mind of God. He custom-designed your body to His specifications and then blessed you with a unique personality and natural gifts and talents – all to fulfill the purpose for which He created you. Knowing this, you should begin to understand that your life has profound meaning. The significance of your existence is far greater than your heart and mind can probably comprehend. You will not fully understand how significant you are to God and to this world until you know for yourself the specific purpose God had in mind when He created you.

Few of us clearly know our purpose for our being. However, if you are intrigued with the idea of discovering your life purpose, then you are most likely ready to consciously live the life God purposed for you. Begin asking yourself the right questions and the right answers will come. You will never discover your life purpose focusing on yourself. Asking questions like, *"Who do I want to be? What should I do with my life? What are my dreams?"*, will not work. Turn to God for answers. Seek Him and His Word. Build your life on eternal truths. Self-help, motivational and inspirational stories and books cannot help you. Within time, God will reveal your purpose to you providing you with the answer to one of life's most important questions: What on earth am I here for?

Knowing your life's purpose and fully living it will bring much meaning and fulfillment into your life. When you consciously align with your true purpose for existing, you will tap into rich reserves of energy, personal power and passion. Your life will begin to flow in new and delightful ways, giving meaning to your life. Without purpose, life has no meaning. With purpose, every day is a reason to live. Even in the midst of life's storms, you will be able to hold on, believing God when He said, *"I know the thoughts that I think toward you...thoughts of peace, and not of evil, to give you an expected end."* Knowing your purpose simplifies your life; it tells you which activities are important, and which are not. You will not be moved to react based on circumstances, pressures, or your feelings. As a result, your life will become focused. You will not be distracted by minor issues, but you will live on purpose, avoiding the stresses of life.

Your character, faith, love, obedience, integrity, and loyalty will be developed as you will be tested by major changes, delayed promises, undeserved criticism, senseless tragedies and possibly more. However, do not be dismayed, for you must be like the repellent, unassuming caterpillar that does not resist change when the time comes to enter the dark cocoon, but accepts it as the next step to transformation and beautification. When the caterpillar first enters the cocoon, its skin is shed then dissolved, leaving a soft, rubbery form called a chrysalis. If you were to peek inside the cocoon, you would only see a puddle of gooey substance. But in that substance are certain cells that contain the DNA-coded instructions for turning the caterpillar goo into a beautiful butterfly. Using the caterpillar as your example, you must allow your old identity to dissolve in the cocoon of God's love so that He can transform you into the beautiful, purpose-filled woman He destined you to be. Your life will flourish readying you for eternity.

Never forget that your time here on earth is temporal and it is imperative that you give God glory in all that you do while you are here. Everyday should be treated as an opportunity to glorify God by worshipping Him, by loving and serving others, by endeavoring to be Christ like, and by witnessing to others about God's great and abiding love. One day you will stand before God and it will be He who determines whether you fulfilled your life purpose and are, therefore, worthy to enter into His kingdom. Show forth your steadfast belief that your life really isn't about you. It's about God, who created you for His purpose and for His glory.

SEASONED SALT

Points to Ponder:

- ➢ Focusing on ourselves will never reveal our life's purpose.
- ➢ Without God, life makes no sense.
- ➢ God is not haphazard. He created us and planned our lives with great precision.
- ➢ Living on purpose is the path to peace.
- ➢ Life is a test, life is a trust, and life is a temporary assignment.
- ➢ Living for God's glory is the greatest achievement we can accomplish with our lives.

Questions to Consider:

1. Knowing that God uniquely created me, what areas of my personality, background, and physical appearance am I struggling to accept?

   _____

   _____

2. What would my family and friends say is the driving force of my life? What do I want it to be?

   _____

   _____

3. What has happened to me recently that I now realize was a test from God?

   _____

   _____

4. What can I do to help me prepare for and pass the tests God will put before me?

   _____

   _____

5. How should the fact that life on earth is just a

temporary assignment change the way I am living right now?

_____

_____

6. What one thing can I start doing today that will bring glory to God?

_____

_____

Identifying Who You Are

Man was created to worship God. The need to connect with Him is inherent in our character. However, if we choose not to worship Him, we will ultimately find a substitute to worship, whether it is a material possession, a man or ourselves. Those who do not have true knowledge of God will worship anything and, as a result, they develop a sinful nature and become trapped in diverse evils, vices, and violations. Scripture instructs us to *"...worship the Lord thy God, and him only shalt thou serve."*

In short, to worship God means to give Him pleasure. In fact, anything you do that brings pleasure to God is an act of worship. Isn't it wonderful to know that your acts of worship bring a smile to the face of God? He actually takes great pleasure and smiles upon you when you worship Him to the point where you love Him supremely, trust Him completely, obey Him wholeheartedly, use the abilities He gave you, praise and thank Him continually.

To worship God effectively you must remember that the key to worship is surrender. Many of us have a tendency to equate surrender with defeat and losing, making it difficult to surrender to God. We must surrender to Him or offer ourselves completely to Him in order to worship Him. You cannot surrender to God unless you can trust Him; trust that God loves you and that He wants the best for you. Admit your limitations. As humans we have limitations and cannot be in control of everything, so we must come to the point of complete surrender and allow God to be God in our lives.

Surrendering to God will allow Him to do His greatest work in you. Do not be afraid of the unknown, for nothing under God's control is out of control. Do not allow your fears, self-will, pride, or personal ambitions to hinder you from receiving God's blessing. Surrendering to God will also allow you to develop a friendship with Him. He desires to be your best friend. Jesus said, *"Henceforth I call you not servants; for the servant knoweth not what his Lord doeth: but I have called you friends: for all things that I have heard of my Father I have made known unto you."* Jesus uses the word friend in this verse to denote a close, trusted relationship, not a casual acquaintance. Through constant conversation with Him about every aspect of your life and through continual meditation upon His Word throughout the day, you can develop a close friendship with God.

However, you must remember that friendships can be tested by separation and silence. In your friendship with God, the time will come when it will seem as though He has abandoned you. It is at these times that worship is most difficult, and you may begin to feel that something is wrong with you or that you've committed a sin against God. Though sin does separate us from intimate fellowship with God, oftentimes the feeling of abandonment has nothing to do with sin and everything to do with your faith being tested. To endure these times of separation, tell God how you feel, focus on His unchanging nature, trust that He will keep His promises and reflect on the things He's already done for you. Do not allow yourself to believe that He has given up on you. Meditate on the scripture that says, *"for he hath said, I will never leave thee, nor forsake thee."*

The worship of God is the exaltation of God. He receives the honor and the glory that is due to Him. In return, grace and blessings descend upon you. *"For the Lord taketh pleasure in His people; he will beautify the meek with salvation."*

Points to Ponder:

- ➤ We were planned to bring pleasure to God through an act of worship.
- ➤ God smiles when we:
    a. love Him supremely
    b. trust Him completely
    c. obey Him wholeheartedly
    d. praise and thank Him continually
    e. use our abilities
- ➤ The heart of worship is surrender.
- ➤ God desires to be our best friend.
- ➤ We should long to have a friendship with God.
- ➤ When we feel abandoned by God yet continue to trust Him, we worship Him in the deepest way.

Questions to Consider:

1. Knowing that the Bible says that all that I do should be to the glory of God, what common task could I start doing as if I were doing it directly for God?

   _____

   _____

2. Since God knows what is best, in what areas of my life do I need to trust Him most?

   _____

   _____

3. Which is more pleasing to God right now - my public worship or my private worship? What will I do about this?

   _____

   _____

4. How can I stay focused on God's presence, especially when He feels distant?

   _____

   _____

5. Knowing that bitterness is the greatest barrier to friendship with God, what can I do to strengthen my friendship with God in spite of the things that seem to be going wrong in my life?

_____

_____

Shaped for Serving God

You were created to serve God and He is worthy of your service simply because of who He is. Having always existed, He is eternal. His power is seen in the vastness of the universe. His wisdom is manifested in its complex design. He is the Almighty whose purposes cannot be limited. He is infinitely wise and His ways are past finding out. The exceeding riches of His grace are breathtaking, and the gift of His Son to redeem rebellious humanity provides ample motive for all to surrender in service to Him.

Nevertheless, you should not serve God out of guilt, fear or a sense of duty. Instead, serve Him with unrestraint joy and deep gratitude because of His goodness toward you. When your life here on earth comes to an end, you will stand before God to be evaluated on your level of service toward Him. How well you served your purpose will also be determined by how well you served others.

Your service toward others lies in your purpose or assignment God gave specifically to you to fulfill. When He gave you the assignment, He also equipped you with certain capabilities to fulfill it. The custom-designed combination of those capabilities are known as your SHAPE:

- **S**piritual Gifts - Your gifts were given to you to serve others, not yourself.
- **H**eart - Serve God from the heart, with passion.
- **A**bilities - Use the abilities God has given you to glorify Him.
- **P**ersonality - Your personality is just right for serving God; all types of personalities are needed in the Body of Christ.
- **E**xperience - God uses your experiences in life to prepare you for ministry.

God has uniquely shaped you for your purpose. Your purpose is to do what God created you to do. You are here to serve God and you serve Him by serving others. Your service is your ministry. Though many confuse ministers with pastors, the truth is everyone is a minister. Whenever you use your gifts and talents to help others, you are ministering.

You are going to dedicate your life to something. Why not dedicate it to serving God? While commitment to a career, fame, and wealth will not have lasting significance, service will result in lasting significance. Furthermore, service is not optional or voluntary. To be a child of God, you must be committed to a life of serving others.

Many have vowed to live a life of service, but in reality they are giving God their second best. They have so little time for God and others. Still they expect God's grace to be with them and for Him to give them the desires of their hearts. They do not realize they are serving God with a spirit of mediocrity and that they are not thinking like a real, mature servant.

To be a real servant of God, you must think like a servant: real service starts in the mind. Real servants are anxious to serve and make themselves available to God anytime. Real servants are always attentive to the needs of others. Real servants are faithful and dependable and complete every task with the same dedication. They do not seek attention. They are content to serve in obscurity.

Real servants also understand that God uses their weaknesses to show Himself strong in their life of service to others. If you can admit that God works best when you are weak, God will abundantly bless you and use you in a great way as you live a life of service to Him and others.

Paul referred to his weakness as a thorn- a limitation in his life over which he had no power to change. Like God mightily used Paul, He will use you if you allow Him to use your weakness for His glory. You can yield your weakness to God by doing what Paul did.

- *Admit your weaknesses*
- *Be content with your weaknesses*
- *Honestly share your weaknesses*

Points to Ponder:

- Service is the pathway to real significance and it is not optional.
- We were shaped and molded for serving God.
- God divinely shapes our abilities, personality and experiences individually and uniquely.
- God deserves our best.
- Serving others requires maturity.
- Service starts in our minds.
- Our most effective ministry will come out of our deepest hurt.
- God works best when we admit our own weaknesses.

Questions to Consider:

1. What is holding me back from God's call to serve Him?

   _____

   _____

2. How does comparing myself to others keep me from fully developing my unique shape?

   _____

   _____

3. What God-given ability or personal experience can I offer to my church?

   _____

   _____

4. How can I make the best use of what God has given me?

   _____

   _____

5. Am I usually more concerned about being served or finding ways to serve others?

6. Am I limiting God's power in my life by trying to hide my weaknesses?

_____

_____

7. How have I seen God's power demonstrated through me when I have felt weak?

_____

_____

We Were Formed for God's Family

Having the Holy Spirit within us is the true essence of what it means to be a Christian. *"Now if any man have not the Spirit of Christ, he is none of his."* Furthermore, if you have Christ in you, your life will be changed and live like Him. As a result of having the Spirit of Christ, we have a new relationship with God; we are members of His family. Apostle Paul declares, *"For as many as are led by the Spirit of God, they are the sons of God."* Paul then goes on to speak of us as "children," "heirs," and "co-heirs with Christ," and he assures us that we are God's children by the new birth, having the status of adopted children.

It should be noted, however, that not everyone is a member of God's family. Having been created by God makes us all His creatures, but only those who are "led by the Spirit of God" can be deemed as the sons, or children, of God. Even Jesus said, *"If God were your father, ye would love me...He that is of God heareth God's words; ye therefore hear them not, because ye are not of God."*

There is no higher honor or greater privilege than being a member of God's family. The moment you were reborn through Christ into God's family, you received the family name, the family likeness, family privileges, family intimate access, and the family inheritance. In other words, you became an heir of God through Christ.

One of the most wonderful dynamics of being in God's family is that we are all His children, without distinction of race, social status, gender, or degree of personal holiness. As Christians we must defy notions of distinction that cause us to think that sin and weaknesses in others make them lesser members of God's family. What matters most is that we love one another as God has loved us.

God is love and if you have God in you, you will love as He does. Giving love and special attention to others in the family of God should be one of your top priorities. Life is all about love, for life without love is worthless because it is eternal and everlasting. God will evaluate you on your love because God measures the level of your spiritual maturity by the quality of your relationships.

The family of God consists of many newly saved members. Many of them are carnal Christians, which means they do not have a mature spiritual life and are childish when it comes to the things of God. They require much patience and kindness. As members of the same family, God expects you to be committed to loving them. Love, support and assist them in developing into mature Christians who, in turn, will love and support other newly saved Christians.

It is for this reason God promotes fellowship among believers. Believers love, support, and encourage each other. Your local church is a good place to start seeking out other believers to whom you can show love and support.

The local church is not only a place of fellowship for

young Christians, but for those who are seasoned Christians as well. We all need a church family. Many benefits come with being committed and active in a local church:

- Having a church family helps you to focus less on yourself and more on loving others.
- Having a church family helps you to learn from other believers and thereby grow in the things of God.
- Having a church family will provide you with a place to discover, develop, and use your spiritual gifts.
- Having a church family will allow you to be a part of a body that will share Christ's mission in the world.
- Having a church family will provide you with a support group of believers who will act as your accountability partners.

So it becomes clear that being a part of a local church is crucial to your walk with the Lord. It is, therefore, important that you protect the unity of your church. God's desire is that you experience a spirit of unity - a spirit of harmony and oneness - with other members of your church. By focusing on commonalities among members, remaining realistic in your expectations of others, encouraging rather than criticizing, shunning gossip, and practicing conflict resolution, you can do your part to protect the unity in your church, for without unity among believers, true fellowship cannot exist.

We Were Created to Become Like Christ

God created you to be like Christ. Like Christ bears His image, God wants His children to bear his image as well. This doesn't mean that you will become God, or even a god. It means that you will be *godly* endowed with God's values, attitudes, and character. The Scripture tells us *"to put off the old man, which is corrupt according to the deceitful lusts, so that we can be renewed in the spirit of our mind"*. We are then instructed to put on the new man, which after God, is created in righteousness and true holiness. His desire is for you to mature spiritually and be transformed into the image of Christ.

In order to be transformed, we require truth. The process of transforming us into the image of Christ is called sanctification and Jesus prayed for God *"to sanctify us through His truth, for God's Word is truth"*. So, it is God's Word that reveals truth to us that we might be made like his Son. Therefore, you must accept the Bible as the authority by which you set your standards and not by unreliable authorities such as culture, tradition, reason, or emotions. You must also incorporate Biblical truths into your life by receiving them, reading, researching, remembering, and reflecting upon them. Then put those truths into practice. As the Scripture says, *"we must become doers of the Word and not hearers only"*. Though the truth will ultimately transform you and set you free, the truth can initially be difficult and painful.

When you live by God's truth, He will begin the process of transforming you. When God's Word begins to expose your faults and sins, it can cause you to feel miserable. It's during those moments that you must remember to press on through the change process if you want to be like Christ. The same is true when you encounter problems in your life. Problems come to make you look to God for answers and not within yourself. Work through your problems, remember that God has a purpose behind every problem. *"And we know that all things work together for good to them that love God, to them who are the called according to his purpose."*

Many times the problems you encounter will be in the form of temptation. Satan uses temptation as a weapon to destroy you, but God wants to use it to help you grow. So whenever you make the choice to resist the temptation instead of yielding to sin, your character is being developed to be like Christ.

Everyone is subject to temptation, and temptation comes back again and again, even after you resist it. Someone once asked, "Why is it that opportunity knocks only once, but temptation knocks persistently?" It continues to return because Satan uses the same old tricks and strategies to terminate your walk with the Lord.

One thing is for sure...temptation is a topic we are all familiar with and could use help overcoming. Understanding how temptation works can help you in overcoming it. Below are specific steps you can take to overcome temptation:

- *Refuse to be intimidated by temptation.* You will never grow to the point where you are never tempted, and it is not a sin to be tempted; temptation becomes sin only when you yield to it.

- *Recognize your pattern of temptation and be prepared for it.* It is important for you to identify the situations and circumstances in which you are most vulnerable to temptation and avoid them as much as possible. The Enemy knows your weaknesses and he will take advantage of every opportunity to tempt you with them.

- *Request God's help.* Do not fail to cry out to God when you're tempted. He wants to help you defeat temptation regardless of the number of times you might have given in to it before, for His love is everlasting.

If you want to overcome temptation, you can, because there is always a way out of temptation. When confronted with temptation, you can defeat it if you remember to refocus your attention on something else. Communicating with a godly person or group about your struggle with the persistent temptation can also help. Resist the Devil with the Word of God and understand that you are vulnerable to temptation and avoid it. You will find that when you defeat temptation, you will grow spiritually. Remember that there are no shortcuts to becoming a mature Christian. It takes time to develop a Christlike character and if you are patient and persistent, God will transform you into the image of Christ.

Points to Ponder:

- Being included in God's family is the highest honor and the greatest privilege we will ever receive.
- Life is all about love.
- The greatest gift we can give someone is our time.
- We discover our role in life through our relationships with others.
- We need others in our life.
- Cultivating a community requires commitment.
- We are called to reconcile, restore and rebuild.
- It is the responsibility of the believer to protect the unity of the church.
- The way we think determines the way we feel and the way we feel influences the way we act.
- Truth transforms us.
- There is a purpose behind every problem.
- Every temptation is an opportunity to do good.
- Maturity and growth takes time. There are no shortcuts.

Questions to Consider:

1. How can I start treating other believers as members of my own family?

   _____

   _____

2. Does my level of involvement in my local church demonstrate that I love and am committed to God's family?

   _____

   _____

3. What are the most common excuses people give for not joining a church, and how would I answer them?

   _____

   _____

4. Who do I need to restore a broken relationship with today?

   _____

   _____

5. What am I personally doing to protect unity in my church family right now?

6. In what area of my life do I need to ask for the Spirit's power to be like Christ today?

7. What has God already told me in His Word that I haven't started doing yet?

8. What problem in my life has caused the greatest growth in me?

9. What Christlike character can I develop by defeating the most common temptation I face?

Linking Your Purpose and Mission

When we are filled with God and can worship Him, it is then that we can go before His throne of sovereign grace and find the reality of His glory – the purpose for which He created us.

You were created for a purpose and there is absolutely nothing in this world that will bring you as much joy and fulfillment as knowing the purpose behind your creation and embracing that purpose with your whole heart, mind, soul, and strength.

Your purpose and your mission are intertwined. Both point to the assignment God has given you to complete while you are here on earth. In fact, He has given you both a mission and a ministry. Your mission involves service to unbelievers, while your ministry is service to believers. Together, your mission and ministry establish your life mission.

For many reasons your life mission is important:

- Your mission is a continuation of Jesus' mission on earth.
- Your mission is a wonderful privilege.

- Your mission is one of the greatest goals you can accomplish.
- Your mission has eternal significance.
- Your mission gives your life meaning.
- Your mission is connected to God's timetable for history's conclusion.

God wants you to accept His mission for your life because He desires to speak through you. He wants you to share with others the life message He has given you. Your life message consists of the following four parts:

- Your testimony: the story of how you came to confess Jesus as your personal Lord and Savior,
- Your life lessons: the lessons God has taught you about Him, relationships, problems, and other aspects of life,
- Your godly passions: the things God has made you to care about most,
- The Good News: the message that God loved us so much that He sent His Son to redeem us from our sins.

When you share your life message, you are carrying out the Great Commission. This commission is your commission. It was given to every follower of Christ, not just to pastors and evangelists. Choosing to become a Christian is a great choice. We all tend to be drawn to the purposes we have more passion for and disregard the others. Having balance in your life helps to eliminate that tendency. Below are four habits Christians should develop in order to keep balance in their lives:

- Talk issues over with a spiritual partner or small group
- Give yourself a spiritual examination periodically
- Record your progress in a journal
- Share the things you've learned with others

Christians who maintain a balanced life are ready to live on purpose. This is really the only way to live. When we lose this perspective, the power of the redemption - the life, death and resurrection of Jesus Christ - loses its ability to draw sinners to Christ. When we fail to passionately embrace the glory of God, we contribute to the distortion of God's work of redemption. We must remember that any and all mission endeavors will fall short when those carrying out the missions are not passionate about pursuing God's glory first in their personal lives.

Points to Ponder:

- ➤ God created me to carry out a specific mission.
- ➤ The Great Commission was given to every follower of Jesus Christ.
- ➤ God desires to speak through us.
- ➤ We must have balance in our lives.
- ➤ We must strive to live on purpose.

SEASONED SALT

Questions to Consider:

1. What fears have kept me from fulfilling the mission God made me to accomplish?

   _____

   _____

2. What keeps me from telling others the Good News?

   _____

   _____

3. As I reflect on my personal story, who does God want me to share it with and why?

   _____

   _____

4. What is the name of an unbelieving friend that everyone in the group can start praying for?

   _____

   _____

SEASONED SALT

5. What steps can I take to start sharing my Life Message with others?

_____

_____

6. What can I do to ensure that I will keep balance in my life and continue to live on purpose?

_____

_____

A Woman
and
Her God

Prayer is important, and you have to know how to pray in order to walk this path. In this section we will assist you with understanding how to structure your prayers to make them more effective.

A Prayer That Changes Things

The Model Prayer

"Our Father which art in heaven,
Hallowed be thy name.
Thy kingdom come.
Thy will be done in earth,
as it is in heaven.
Give us this day our daily bread.
And forgive us our debts,
as we forgive our debtors.
And lead us not into temptation,
but deliver us from evil:
For thine is the kingdom, and the power,
and the glory, forever.
Amen."

Matthew 6:9-13

The model prayer, sometimes called The Lord's Prayer, is perhaps the most recited prayer in the world. It also has the distinction of being the first prayer *taught* to the disciples of Jesus Christ. Within this distinction, we often overlook a key word, "taught." The disciples were *taught* how to pray. This indicates prayer is a practice that is not automatically known; one must learn. In learning *how* to pray, one cannot rely on *hearing* the prayers of our grandmothers, fathers, and pastors, nor can one learn by *viewing* the many prayers written in books, pamphlets and other Christian literature. One learns to pray by doing. And in doing, we not only learn how to pray but also, we develop our prayers into successful, effective, strong prayers.

Why is learning how to pray successful prayers important? Because as you go through the process of changing into the woman God wants you to be, you will experience very painful days, months, even years. Prayers change things, people or situations. Change is not painless. Change can breed uncertainty, fear, depression, anger, hopelessness, and the list goes on. It will be necessary during this time of change to stay close to God in prayer so that He can revive you, give you hope and love you.

The Model Prayer

Our Father in heaven, Hallowed be Your name.

This is the first secret of a successful prayer. Pray to the right and only source. Pray to the One who has all power and authority; pray to the One who controls the heavens, the universe and all that is in it; pray to the One who sits high and looks low.

If you grew up in a family with multiple children, your mother, at some time or another, wanted your attention. In her distraction—mothers are very distracted creatures—she probably called you your brother or sister's name. If she did, you didn't answer, thinking she wanted your brother or sister. When she finally got to your name, the right name, that's when you perked up, listened to her and scurried off to attend to her request. This is the same operating principle for our Father in heaven. Direct your prayers to someone other than Him, the Supreme Being, and He will not listen. God is a gentleman; He will not eavesdrop on someone else's conversation. But, in directing your prayer to Him, He promises in his Word, He will not only hear but also hasten to heed your call.

Inherent in the opening of The Model Prayer, is the subtle acknowledgement that God is the ultimate giver of all things. Why pray to someone or something that can't hear you, do for you or fellowship with you? Why repeat the sins of those who prayed to Baal or the Greek gods or the king or saints? Successful prayers are those directed to the One who controls everything. Successful prayers are directed to God, who has all power and authority and commands all things.

The final point to be made regarding the opening sentence of prayer is that God should be approached with reverence and praise. His Word tells us, *we should enter His gates with thanksgiving, And into His courts with praise.* All praise, glory and honor belong to Him and Him alone. There is none worthier of our highest praise than God Almighty! When we call on Him with sweet, sweet words, it is pleasing to Him; it's inviting to Him; it stirs Him to come down from His high throne and bless us with His presence. God is worthy, worthy of all praise! Hallelujah!

Your kingdom come.

The second sentence of prayer expresses God's agenda as spoken by Jesus and to be modeled by us. God begot His only son and sent Him to live among us so that we might experience the essence of Him—His love and goodness—through His son. The disciples were a blessed group to live and breathe God's image in the flesh (Jesus). But, that same opportunity exists for us today simply by *asking* God into our hearts and then by allowing Him to *control* our thoughts, our words, our deeds, our actions. In this way, we can still advance the kingdom of God even in these trouble-riddled, contemporary times.

Jesus also tells us that God's agenda is to save a dying world. It is not enough to experience Him and adopt His ways. Those committed to God make it their business to be about His business of pouring the love and image of Jesus Christ into *all* men, women, and children. The key to successful prayer is to pray that all God's people come to know and emulate his character. Those who are wholly committed to God's agenda will pray unselfishly that all people come to know and model Jesus in their hearts. Those who want God's kingdom advanced will pray unselfishly for those who do not have a connection to God. Those who want successful prayers will pray unselfishly for those who are separated from the love of God. And the bonus for you is that you will experience the joy of effective praying while also marveling at how God meets all your needs. For when you are about your Father's business, He is handling yours! Praise God!

Your will be done on earth as it is in heaven.

Closely connected to advancing God's kingdom is praying for God to have His way in our natural world. If you want successful, effective prayers, pray the words of this traditional hymn, "*Have thine own way, Lord. Have thine own way. You are the potter; I am the clay.*"

It takes courage to pray those words. For when you do, you are opening yourself to be led by the Spirit without foresight or a game plan or map. And for many people, that is scary. It is human nature to want at least some idea of what's down the road. Yet, in giving God full control, in praying that His will be done on earth, we remove the need to have a five or even a one-year plan and trust God to take good care of everything...and us.

Rest assured, there is no cause for fear when in His Word, we are encouraged to, *"Ask, and it will be given to you; seek, and you will find; knock, and it will be opened to you."* If you want to know the will of God, speak to Him openly, honestly, and freely. In fact, God is pleased when we come to Him with an open heart and eager spirit. It makes Him smile; it makes Him happy.

So the next time you pray, go to a still, silent place, become calm and meditative, then ask the presence of God to touch you, to come into your heart. Resist the urge to rattle off your needs, like a supercharged "to-do" list. Resist the worries of the day that will try and break through this time of peace. Instead, remain focused on the presence of the Holy Spirit and pray. Your prayer: unselfish concern for God's plan for all of Creation!

Give us this day our daily bread.

There are several reasons Jesus did not say, "give us this *month* our daily bread." Can you guess what those reasons are?

Write your answer here.

If you wrote, "to encourage His people to speak with Him on a daily basis," you guessed correctly. Both the Father and Son are intimately aware of the demands of our day. Commutes to work, child care issues, financial shortages, faltering health, decisions to be made, tiredness, home repair problems...this is just a short list of the daily worries that weigh us down and cause us to miss out on time with God.

Successful, effective prayers require spending daily time with God. How else can we expect to know His will? How else can we pray for the lost and confused, the poor in spirit? How else can we thank Him, praise Him, rejoice in His goodness? As women desiring to change into beautiful butterflies, it is imperative that we seek His face daily...if for no other reason than to keep us from failing this change. Don't let the cares of this world crowd out your daily talk with Jesus. Just to feel His presence, to receive His touch is enough to rejuvenate and recharge us so we can breeze through the day.

Now, if you guessed (in response to the question above) that daily contact provides us the opportunity to increase our trust in and dependence on God, you, too, are correct. The children of Israel, while wandering in the wilderness, were pleased and surprised to receive manna and quail from God.

In forty years of wandering in the wilds, their clothes did not wear out and their sandals held strong. Their daily needs were met. God wants to do the same for us. He is willing and more than able to work out all your concerns, problems and issues while you take sweet rest in His comforting arms. Try Him! Ask Him to supply your daily needs. Test Him! Hand over your daily cares to Him. Then sit back, observe and be like the children of Israel—awed!

By now you realize the word bread as originally quoted by Jesus has been expanded to "needs." Our needs, whether they be emotional, physical, spiritual, great or small, is what Jesus references in his prayer. Because Jesus is not a limited Savior we should not limit what we take to God in prayer. Trust Him with every need and learn for yourself how wonderful, caring, smart and creative God is.

Give your all to His altar and come to appreciate all the many names we ascribe to Him. Spend time with Him, starting today.

And forgive us our debts, as we forgive our debtors.

Jesus often taught in parables and allegories, at times using words that symbolized or stood in place for something else. This holds true in His model prayer. The word "debts" should not be thought of in terms of money or finances only. In fact, when we unearth the true meaning of the word we understand it relates to "our heart condition." Let's shed more light on this definition, using one of Jesus' parables...the parable of the servant.

A certain servant owed a great sum of money to his king. In Matthew 18:23-34, the indebted servant, when called before the king for reckoning, asks for forgiveness of his debt because he cannot pay. The king, in his infinite mercy and goodness, forgives the servant of the money owed and releases him to freedom. However, the same servant goes immediately in search of one who owes him money. He finds one and demands payment, even to the point of becoming physical. The one cannot pay and the servant has him thrown in jail. When the king hears of the servant's unforgiving and hard heart, he has the servant thrown in jail until his debt is paid in full.

As you can see, the servant had a bad heart condition. He had the opportunity to forgive as he had been forgiven, but he didn't. He had the chance to show mercy; he didn't. He could have displayed great Jesus-like characteristics, but instead he operated in the natural and ended up reaping what he sowed. If you do not want to be like the ungrateful servant, then forgive those who hurt, harm, and dismiss you. Practice mercy and kindness at all times. No, it's not easy. Our instinct, as humans, is to strike out after being struck. In our humanness, we hold on to anger and grudges and bitterness. That's why it is so important to stay in daily touch with God.

We need His grace to fall fresh on us every day. We need to be washed in the blood of the Lamb every day. We need His love and presence daily so we can ask for forgiveness of our sins and in turn, extend forgiveness and love to others. Do not let unforgiveness, anger, bitterness, contempt, hatred and other "bad heart conditions" get in the way of your successful prayers. Every day, pray for God's mercy and forgiveness, then leave your communion place, adopting a forgiving spirit, a loving countenance, and allowing the Spirit of the Lord to be your guide in matters requiring heart.

And do not lead us into temptation, but deliver us from the evil one.

This sixth sentence of Jesus' prayer is a proactive command that, if followed, allows us to keep pain, heart ache and trouble at bay or at least at a minimum. However, if not followed, there's still good news...it will provide us with a solution or a way out of any problem or situation.

As long as we live and breathe, the devil will tempt us just as he tempted Jesus. The key to overcoming the wiles of the devil is preparation through praying. Just a simple prayer such as, "Lord, keep me strong and in your will," goes a long way in deflecting the darts of temptation. Such a simple prayer builds a hedge of protection around you, causing temptation to fall by the wayside without you even lifting a finger and sometimes without you even being aware of the temptation.

Now that's good news! But, unfortunately, we don't always pray the prayer of preparation and protection. When this happens, Jesus, in His infinite wisdom, has already provided for us. He prayed the second part, *"...deliver us from evil,"* for those times when temptation slays us, we curse the driver who cuts us off in traffic, we scream and yell at our child who has brought home another sub-standard report card, we over drink, over eat, over talk, etc. For those times when we give in to the flesh, we can go to the Father, in our deepest regret and with sickness of heart, and ask for forgiveness. We ask our Father to help us be strong in the face of temptation and to provide a way out of it. Our Father in heaven, who hears, will grant our request.

Thank God, Jesus taught us to anticipate temptation and pray for covering! Thank God, victorious living can be ours! Hallelujah!!

> *For Yours is the kingdom*
> *and the power and the glory forever.*
> *Amen.*

In closing a successful prayer, we are ever careful of ending like we begin, in praise and adoration of the one and only King, in awe and reverence to the Lord of Lords, in thanksgiving and acknowledgment of His eternal power and everlasting kingdom.

How great it is that we, sinners, saved by grace, have direct access to God and all His good and perfect gifts. How wonderful it is to know that He cares for us and is with us all the days of our lives. What a mighty God we serve! He alone is worthy!

God Answers

We have spent time reviewing The Model Prayer because it is *the* model for successful prayers. When we incorporate His prayer into our daily prayers, we open ourselves to receive indescribable joy and peace. We also position ourselves to hear from the Lord. God will answer your prayers. Sometimes He answers right away; sometimes it takes months, even years. But rest assured, He *will* respond. Let's examine some of God's ways of answering prayers.

Three Possible Responses from God

| No/Wait | Yes | Grace and Mercy |

No/wait. What can be more disappointing or frustrating than being told, 'no' and/or 'wait' by God? When God answers in this way, we tend to respond like children. We beg, plead, hold our breath, or resort to the silent treatment. We may even try bribing God or question His authority or speculate about his feelings toward us. But unlike children, we come to understand God's no/wait is a good thing. We realize a no/wait can be translated into "I've got something better for you." "That's not what I want for you." "It's not for your good." "This is my (God's) will."

God's no/wait can mean He's allowing the right details and circumstances to come together. It could mean you're not ready yet to receive what He has for you or perhaps this period is a special time of testing. Maybe God wants to see your faith in action and/or take note of your obedience. Regardless of God's reason for the no/wait, we come to understand we cannot conceive all that God has planned for us nor do we know the Master's plan. With this understanding comes our response—rejoice in the Lord, thank Him for His loving care, praise Him through it all and most of all, we hold steady in our prayers.

YES! What more can be said! Either you are praying in God's will or the timing of your prayer coincides with God's timing. Regardless the reason, you get what God purposed for you to have. And here's a little secret... Because He is a good God, He delights in giving even more that we asked for! An overflowing blessing. Hallelujah!!!

Grace and Mercy. The twin gifts are just that... gifts. God freely gives grace and mercy to His children, the believing body. There's nothing we can do to earn the gifts, nothing we can pay to purchase these gifts. Indeed, when God sacrificed His Son's life for humanity and when we confess Jesus as our Lord and Savior, we inherit the gifts of grace and mercy.

God's answer of *"my grace is sufficient"* usually comes in circumstances that appear hopeless or unfair. We focus not on the situation but on God's gifts. We thank Him for those gifts, which give us the strength to endure, and we thank Him for His unconditional love.

Pray According to His Word

The recommended way of prayer is to speak boldly the Words (scripture) of God to God. Why? Because every word of God is pure. Use His Word and expect to be blessed.

Roman 12:1: *Heavenly father, according to your word, I present my body a living sacrifice holy, and acceptable to you.*

Eph. 6:14-17: *Now, Father, I gird my loins about with truth, I put on the breastplate of righteousness, I shod my feet with the preparation of the gospel of peace. Above all, I take the shield of faith wherewith I shall be able to quench all the fiery darts of the wicked. And I take the helmet of salvation, and the sword of the Spirit, which is the Word of God.*

Isa. 58:8: *And, according to your Word, the glory of the*

Lord is my rear guard.

Isa. 61:3: *Now, Heavenly Father, I put on the garment of praise, and I thank you for the armor you have provided for me to dress in this day. I am completely covered now, in the name of Jesus, according to your Word.*

Matt. 16:18: *Upon Jesus I have built my life, my home and my family, and the gates of hell shall not prevail against it.*

Ps. 23:1: *You are my shepherd; I shall not want.*

Phil. 4: 19 & Phil. 4: 13: *For you have supplied all my need according to your riches in glory and I can do all things through Christ, who strengthens me.*

2 Cor. 10:5 & 1 Pet. 5:17: *Cast down all imagination and bring into captivity every evil thought, and I cast all my cares upon you, for you care for me.*

Ps. 103:3 & Isa. 53:5: *I praise you that I walk in divine health, for you are my God who heals all my diseases, and by your stripes I am healed.*

3 John 2: *I praise and thank you for my prosperity and good health, even as my soul prospers.*

Neh. 8:10: *For the Joy of the Lord is my strength.*

Jer. 1:12: *Father, I have prayed according to your Word, and you have said you would hasten your word to perform it.*

You're Not in the Cocoon Alone

Twice now in this lesson we have been blessed with two prayers we can model--one, the Words of Jesus as He taught His disciples how to pray and two, the prayer of the righteous one who incorporated the Word of God. A third prayer follows which combined with the other two prayers serves to solidify this lesson in our hearts and minds. This third prayer, written by DaySpring Cards, leaves us with a permanent reminder that Jesus will never leave nor forsake us. He is our trusted friend who prays for us always.

Dear Daughter,

"Prayer is something that has always been
a part of me. I prayed when I needed to
hear my Father's heart, when I was baptized by
John, when I broke bread, and when I blessed the
children. I prayed when facing my darkest hour,
and I prayed as I gave my life upon the cross.
I prayed in public before others, and I prayed alone.
I prayed in the daytime and I prayed at night.
When I prayed with my disciples just before I was
arrested in the garden, you were included in that
prayer. When I taught my disciples how to pray,
it was for your understanding as well. I know that
I am not physically present with you today as I was
with my disciples so many years ago, but my heart
of prayer has not changed. I am praying for you
now because you are mine. My love for you today is
great, and my heart for you is full. I pray peace

SEASONED SALT

over you and blessings upon you. I pray rivers of joy to be within you and to flow out through you. I pray good things over you. I pray that your life will bear much fruit, that you will grow in grace, that your faith will increase, and that you will stand strong until the day that I see you face to face."

Points to Ponder:

- Successful prayer involves connecting with the Holy Spirit.
- Successful prayer involves praying the will of God and using the Holy Spirit to intercede in times when words are too hard to speak.
- When two or three agree in prayer, the power of prayer increases significantly.
- Prayer and fasting are the tools which guard us against temptation, the devil and his forces.
- When we pray in the name of Jesus, all power is available to us. We use that power for the good of humanity, not for selfish reasons.
- God's Word and God's will are bankable. Have faith and believe.

Questions to Consider:

1. Can you think of a time when God told you no and later you realized it was a good "no?"

   _____

   _____

2. How did you feel before you realized what a blessing the "no" was?

   _____

   _____

3. How did you feel afterwards?

   _____

   _____

4. What struggles and temptations do you need to give to God in prayer?

   _____

   _____

5. What's preventing you from doing so?

   _____

   _____

6. What prevents you from spending daily time with God?

_____

_____

7. What are you willing to sacrifice to spend thirty minutes to an hour each day in prayer and meditation?

_____

_____

8. Is there anything or anyone that has first place in your life before God? If so, how do you plan to replace it with God so that your prayers are more effective?

_____

_____

Devotion

How do you fall in love with someone?

1. Spend time together.
2. Share long conversations.
3. Enjoy shared or common interests.
4. Share similar values, morals and views.
5. Physically attracted, spiritually attracted.
6. Complementary personalities and backgrounds.

Now, how do you fall in love with God? Falling in love with God is much easier because He loved us first and His love is unconditional. You guessed it! The exact same way.

Long before the foundation of the earth was formed, God knew you! He knew your birthday, the color of your eyes, the number of hairs on your head. He knew which baby tooth you would lose first and the hairstyle you like most. He knows your favorite scripture, how you like your sunsets, and whether you have a dry or bubbly sense of humor.

God didn't have to know these things about you to fall in love with you. He loved you from the beginning of time. When darkness covered the face of the earth. Even before your parents ever met. God loves you! His love for you is so deeply rooted and strong, He sacrificed His only Son so that you might be saved. He is so enamored with you, He pledges to care for you and never leave you. Now that's real love! That's pure love!

God's love for each of us is so pure, it's unconditional. There are no strings attached to His love, no conditions that must be met to have His love. There's nothing you have to be or do for God to love you. There's nothing that you can say or do to stop Him from loving you. For many people, this is unfathomable; this unconditional love is just not possible, they say. In their fixed minds, they can't imagine a love that free. But such a love does exist in God.

If you aspire (and we all should) to love God with *all* your heart, to become hopelessly devoted to Him, He makes it very clear what we should do. We should make Him number one in our lives. We should worship Him, desire Him, lean on Him, renew ourselves in Him and rest in His loving arms. We should give Him our love, trust, and our praise. We should develop an intimate relationship with Him, a friendship, a loveship.

If you are ready to do these simple "love" things for God, if you are ready to fall in love with or deepen your love for the great, awesome, and holy God, here's how:

1. Schedule a "date" with God.
2. Keep the "date"; let nothing disrupt that appointment.
3. Select a secluded, quiet place.
4. Invite only God—no one else. Give Him your undivided attention.

5. Speak honestly, holding nothing back.

6. You may choose to include in your "date" the Bible, a devotional, and a journal to record your thoughts and prayers. Any combination of these methods or varied use of these methods will keep the love of God fresh and alive.

7. Allow God time to speak to your heart. His voice surrounds you everywhere you go. One of the popular ways in which He speaks is through His Word. He may also communicate through visual or mental images, through songs, speech, or He may even use signs. Reward yourself by being still just a moment longer and waiting for a revelation.

As you're "dating" God and falling in love with Him, you will come to know Him as a loving Father, a Wonderful counselor, a best friend, a protector, a great provider and the list goes on and on. Continue to develop your intimate, warm and honest relationship with Him, and you will come to appreciate all that He is, was and will ever be.

Give God a gift today. Offer Him yourself! Offer Him your love!

Points to Ponder:

- ➢ The first and great Commandment requires we love the Lord with all our heart, souls and mind.
- ➢ Spending time with and communicating with God is the key to falling in love with God.
- ➢ Be committed to maintaining your loveship with God.
- ➢ Being devoted to God increases our faith, our obedience, and makes us better world citizens.
- ➢ Having a relationship with God makes Him real and personal.

Questions to Consider:

1. Are you living the first Commandment? If not, how do you plan to?

   _____

   _____

2. Have you ever had a personal encounter with God? Is God real to you? If not, do you now know how to make God real in your life?

   _____

   _____

3. Is your "date" with God effective?

   _____

   _____

4. If yes, how? If no, what needs to change to make it so?

   _____

   _____

5. Since falling in love with God, how have you changed?

_____

_____

Worshiping in Spirit and Truth

What is Worship?

In previous lessons, we discussed how prayer and devotion is fundamental in establishing a relationship, a loveship with God. We discussed how this loveship is necessary as we transform ourselves into the image of God, as we prepare to step into our purpose, mission, and roles as women of God. There is another fundamental element that accompanies prayer and devotion: it is Worship. Why is worship as necessary as prayer and devotion? What role does worship play in keeping us strong, encouraged and faithful during seasons of growth?

What is worship? Today, if a non-believer asked you to define worship, what would your response be?

Defining worship can be as elusive as defining air. We know what it is. We experience it. We enjoy it. But, how do we put it into words? Well, the task is made easier by knowing the historical and academic usage.

The word worship is rooted in two Latin words, "veneratio" which means divine, reverence, respect and "cultus" which means reverence and respectful treatment. Webster's Ninth New Collegiate Dictionary, 1991, defines worship as, "reverence offered to a divine being or supernatural power." In tying the historical and academic definitions together, we get a clear, simple answer: Worship is the act of showing respect and reverence to God.

Why Worship?

Why should we pay homage to God? Why should we revere and honor Him? We scratch our head because we know the answer, but how do we put such deep emotions and feelings into words? We are also slightly perplexed because we know the answer is both simple and complex *and* both secular and Christian. How do we respond in such a way to make the "why" of worship clear? We decide to take the standard approach. Start with the simple and build from there.

Simply put, it's natural for us to worship. Worship is an innate, instinctual part of our being which we cannot carve out any more than we can carve out an internal organ and yet expect to live. We cannot not worship! God created us for just that purpose! The trouble and danger with the need to worship, though, lies in its secular application. Because it is natural for us to worship, we often worship the wrong thing. A prized rose garden, our luxury car, our alumni organization, our external appearance, our social or business standing, etc.

Knowing how susceptible we are to "wrong" worship, why would God even allow worship to be unrestricted? Why didn't God insert a DNA code that would force us to worship only Him? Our response leads us to the complexity and spirituality of worship. First, it is not God's nature to force or restrict. God is a God of free will and choice. He allows us to do what we want to do while loving and caring for us. God is too much of a gentle God to insert or assert His authority. He prefers that we come to Him freely, offering praise and worship.

Secondly, we as humans can certainly question and seek to understand *all* the whys and how's of God's creations, but the believer understands there are some things we simply will not know until we see the Master's face. The believer trusts God's infinite wisdom, orderly creation and loving nature. That for us is all the answers we need.

Means, Forms, and How to Worship

We understand what worship is and why we worship so now let's look at how we worship. What does worship "look" like? To answer this question, let's go back to the dictionary as a starting point. Webster's Ninth New Collegiate Dictionary, 1991, offers an additional definition for worship. It is "a form of religious practice with its creed and ritual." This is a good beginning, but it leaves out an inexhaustible list of the various means or forms of worship. Nor does it link these means or forms to God, the One whom we should adorn with our love and worship.

In the Christian faith, worship is normally associated with 11:00 a.m. Sunday service. Indeed, that service is often referred to as "worship service." Within the context of this service are various forms of worship. Some of these ways include, but are not limited to: prayer, praise, sermons, liturgies, bodily movements, facial expressions, time, environment, the acts and dress of the priests and participants, music, poetry, dramatic interpretations, vessels, rites such as baptism and Holy Communion, bulletins/programs, signs, symbols, artwork, sacraments, sacrifices, ministries, and dance can bring out joy, compassion, hope, love, goodwill, happiness, tears, humility, and surrender.

As we see, some of these ways are verbal, some are non-verbal, some visible, others not. Some of these ways are old, from Jesus' time, and some are new. Regardless of the classification, what binds all of these diverse forms is they are all valid and acceptable ways to worship God.

Worship, anytime, anyplace. Daily, we believers worship God. When we give money to the beggar on the street, we worship God. When we discipline a child, we reverence God. When we earnestly and lovingly complete the mundane chores—laundry, errands, cleaning, dusting, etc.—of life, we honor God. When we volunteer our time to causes which uplift humanity, we are worshipping. When we do these and other things as if we are doing them for God and as if God is standing right beside us, we worship.

We come to understand the "look of" or how to worship is diverse and in whatever form, must be directed to God. We understand when worshipping it is critical that the flesh be tamed, that praise and thanksgiving reign in our hearts. When we do this, God is sure to be pleased with our worship and will reward us with a healing and renewing touch.

Worship in Spirit and Truth

The heart of John 4: 23 - 24, our key scripture for this

lesson, is true worship. In this scripture, Jesus informs an unnamed woman that the time is *now* for true worshippers to worship in spirit and in truth. What does it mean to worship in spirit and in truth? What is true worship?

In *The Purpose Driven Life,* author, Rick Warren, offers a dazzling response to these questions. He states the heart of true worship is surrender. When we sincerely open ourselves to God, shedding all the falsities we show to others (and ourselves), setting aside all our humanness, falling down before Him in praise and humbleness, we are then worshipping in spirit and truth.

To worship in spirit and truth has nothing to do with the place of worship, the hour of day or even the form of worship. True worship places us spirit to Spirit with God and allows us to share honestly. For many, this is not easy for they know true worship involves tears, the death of rebellion, submission, the letting go of fear, honesty and a great deal of faith.

Witness the biblical example. Jesus, the night before His crucifixion. As He prayed alone, Jesus stripped all flesh away, baring His soul to the Father. He prayed so hard His sweat appeared as blood. Did He cry? Oh, yes! Did He struggle with the Father's plan? Of course! Did He submit to the will of God? Indeed! Did He have faith? Most assuredly! As Christians, we follow Jesus' example and live!

Points to Ponder:

- Worship is for God and God alone.
- Worship is freely given to God in response to His love, goodness and blessings.
- In whatever way we choose to worship, worship should arouse our senses, thereby making us more aware of God's presence and deepening our love for and appreciation of Him.
- True worship exposes us completely to God and equips us to live as Jesus lived.

Questions to Consider:

1. Have you ever felt your worship was dry and without "life"? If so, what did you do to make worship meaningful once again?

   _____

   _____

2. How do you feel about the contemporary forms of worship, such as dance, mime, plays, etc.? Are they Biblical? Created by God? Why or why not?

   _____

   _____

3. What prevents you from fully exposing yourself to God?

   _____

   _____

4. What makes you "hide" from Him?

   _____

   _____

5. Are you now ready for full exposure?

_____
_____

Woman's Formation

*"In the beginning God created the heavens
and the earth..."*
Genesis 1:1

*"And the Lord God formed man of the dust of the
ground, and breathed into his nostrils the breath of life;
and man became a living being."*
Genesis 2:7

*"Then the rib which the Lord God had taken from
man He made into a woman..."*
Genesis 2:22

In the three "In the Beginning" stories—the beginning of creation; the beginning of man and woman—we read that God put more time and effort into creating woman than he did in creating the heavens, earth or man. How do we know this? His Word tells us so. When creating the heavens and earth, God spoke and the action occurred. *In Genesis 2, the creation of man from dust and blew into his nostrils the breath of life and man became a living soul.*

But Woman! In creating us, God went to work! He caused Adam to sleep. He opened Adam's chest and selected a rib. He closed the flesh and fashioned the rib into woman. That's four steps before getting to the "fashioning" step and can you imagine the work that went into the "fashioning" step alone? Can you imagine the time and effort God expended forming woman with all her complexities, needs, requirements and extra body parts out of a single bone? Now, that's work! That's creation! That's worth a **hallelujah!!**

What this extra care in forming woman tells us is that we are fearfully and wonderfully made. It also tells us we are extremely valuable creatures of God. This is under scored by the fact that although we were created last, God did not consider His creation work *done* until we existed! We, women, embrace these three facts—fearfully and wonderfully made; valuable; we complete creation—and use them as our foundation to become godly women in every facet—spiritually, physiologically, and physically—of our lives.

For us to have a positive impact in and on the lives of others, for us to fulfill our purpose, roles and ministry work, for us to be godly women, we must understand how God fashioned us and how to translate those fashionable traits into characteristics the world can benefit from.

First, let's review how God fashioned us. Our understanding is gleaned from Genesis 1 and 2.

God fashioned woman:

- **In His image**: The first creation story in Genesis 1, verse 27, reads, *"So God created man in His own image; in the image of God He created him; male and female He created them."* God is a God of noble character. He is light and goodness; joy and peace. He is loving and pure; gentle and tolerant. God is aware of and connected to all Creation—the heavens, earth, water, animals, greenery, humans, etc.—and He cares for *all* of His Creations. God is all this and more and since we are created in His image, we are all this and more.

- **To be whole**: True, we were created from Adam's rib, making us a part of him, but let us not forget that the rib was removed and the flesh closed up. Hence, God intends for us to be whole, independent beings, able to stand and function with God as our primary source.

- **To be filled with His Spirit**: *"God breathed into his nostrils the breath of life."* This verse in Genesis 2 tells us God's breath, His Spirit lives in us. He is a part of us. Wherever we go, whatever we do, think or act, God participates.

- **On purpose**: God was methodical in making a mate for Adam. In Genesis chapter 2, the second creation story, verses 18 - 22, when the beasts, birds, cattle and every living creature did not satisfy Adam, God continued the creative process until Adam was pleased. God was determined that Adam's mate would be right and proper for him. This tells us that we are not an accident or after thought, but well designed for a specific purpose. It tells us God intended for us to be right and proper and we hold secure in that knowledge.

- **To be submissive:** Just as man bows to God in total surrender to His maker, woman bows to God, her Creator...ready, able and willing to do His will.

- **To be a helper:** Ribs are positioned along the sides of a man, not behind, in front or underneath. We understand then that as a helper we stand beside the man, providing support, care, loyalty and encouragement.

- **To be diverse and creative:** God's diversity is showcased in Genesis 1 and 2 in all that He made and created. Just think about all the varieties of butterflies He made. Just think about all the colors of a butterfly. Just think about all the shapes, lengths and wingspans a butterfly can have. All of this is from God. And, because we are made in His image and He lives in us, we, too, are diverse in our talents and creative in our abilities.

If we delved deeper into scripture, we could uncover some additional fashionable traits to commit to learning, but for the sake of time, we move on, translating the list above into characteristics that today's woman of God should possess. To assist in our translation, we turn to Proverbs.

As Christian women, we know it is not a mistake that the characteristics of a godly woman are depicted in Proverbs for it is *the book* that instructs, provides wisdom and outlines our relationship with God, with others and with ourselves. It is right that we find our model for being a virtuous, fashionable and godly woman there.

What exactly does it mean to be a godly woman? Most of us would define a godly woman as a virtuous woman - the woman described in Proverbs 31. And when we think of the virtuous woman, we think of a woman who is moral, upright, good, strong in character, courageous, and filled with a spirit of excellence and integrity.

Now ask yourself. Can the virtuous woman be defined as a beautiful woman?

Yes, she can. God wants us to be beautiful. Beauty can be defined as the quality attributed to whatever satisfies or pleases the senses or the mind. We know that God is more interested in our inner beauty than any outward appearance of beauty. We also know that outward beauty is vain, for it doesn't last. Inner beauty, which begins in our heart the moment we commit our lives to God is eternal in nature, lasting always.

So as a beautiful, virtuous woman, God has a plan for your life. He has specifically destined you to fulfill a specific purpose. It is for that reason you must seek Him with all of your heart, and make Him the center of your life. When you put Him first in all that you do, He will give you the desires of your heart.

He will take you into His bosom, nurture you until you are transformed in His image, and then release you to fly with newfound wings like the beautiful butterfly destined to discover all of the great things God has in store for your life.

Characteristics of a Virtuous Woman
Proverbs 31: 10 – 31

- Fears the Lord
- Trustworthy
- Does good, not evil
- Works hard
- Looks good and ensures her family looks good
- Confident
- Generous giver; shares; blesses others
- Supports her family's emotional, mental, physical and spiritual needs, especially her mate's
- Strong
- Honorable with integrity
- Feminine, graceful, gentle
- Good natured, cheerful, nice, calm
- Hopeful, optimistic
- Trusts the Lord with her present and future
- Guards her words, speaking only good
- Wise

Be honest. How many of these characteristics do you

possess? Which ones are you struggling with?

It is so important for the women of God to be godly at all times. Sounds impossible doesn't it? May even have you thinking, "*I can't help but get cranky when it's that time of the month. I get stressed when my paycheck doesn't cover all my obligations. I get angry when my husband just sits around after work and doesn't attempt to help with the kids.*" We all have situations or circumstances that "try" our godliness and yes, during those times, it is tough. Sometimes, it's almost impossible to maintain a godly demeanor, but we are to strive to do so anyway.

Why? Because the women in this world who do not have a relationship with God are watching those of us who profess to have a relationship with God. Because the men in this world who do not have a relationship with God are watching those of us who profess to love Jesus Christ. The world is watching, judging and making a decision about their salvation and their relationship with God based on how we present ourselves. Hence, it is our goal, our mission to ensure we think, talk and do in accordance with His image and likeness.

Also, when we yield to temptation and act or speak in ungodly ways, we block the blessings and praises stored for us. We block peace, love, prosperity, kindness, goodwill, security, comfortable housing, stable families, joy, satisfying careers, and much more.

To live is to be tempted, so the next time you are tempted to act in an ungodly, unfashionable way, run to God in prayer. **Our godly woman prayer:** Remove anything that shouldn't be and replace it with that which emulates you, oh God, my help!

Go forth now, virtuous, godly, fashionable woman and receive all that God has for you!

Points to Ponder:

- A godly woman clothes herself in the spiritual identity of God.
- A virtuous woman has an inner beauty that far outshines the most beautiful appearance.
- A woman of noble character is worth far more than jewels.
- Praises, love and blessings shower the path of the godly woman.
- God has destined for me to be a godly woman.
- A virtuous woman is moral, upright, good, strong in character, courageous, and filled with a spirit of excellence and integrity.

SEASONED SALT

Questions to Consider:

1. How do you feel about being man's helper?

   _____

   _____

2. Think of the godly women in your life. What do you admire most about them?

   _____

   _____

3. Is that characteristic one of your challenges? If so, ask them how they developed that characteristic.

   _____

   _____

4. How does the godly woman maintain godliness while seeing to her many responsibilities and duties?

   _____

   _____

5. How does she maintain balance while giving so much of herself to others?

6. What does being a godly woman mean to me?

7. What can I do to become more of a virtuous woman?

8. How important is outward beauty to me?

9. How important is inner beauty?

10. How can I use my experiences to help hurting women?

Growing in God

The Beatitudes

Just like Jesus taught the disciples how to pray, He also taught them how to achieve a spirituality that went beyond what they were currently experiencing. The Beatitudes, as found in Matthew 5, is the instruction Jesus shared with them.

The Beatitudes, named thusly from ancient Hebrew scripts which often began, "Oh, how happy is he who..." or "Blessed is he who..." teach us how to achieve Jesus' level of righteousness. They move us from religion to spirituality; from spiritual poverty to spiritual prosperity; from infancy in Christ to maturity in Christ.

As we continue growing and maturing in our relationship with God, we will embrace The Beatitudes ("Be of this attitude...") and fold them into our daily living.

Blessed are the poor in spirit, for theirs is the kingdom of heaven.

When we think of the word poor, we think of scarcity, unfulfilled needs, begging, lack, poverty. Coupling that sentiment with the word spirit, we understand that Jesus is teaching us to be ever mindful of our human condition. We as humans have a scarcity of love and needs we cannot meet. We lack joy and peace at times. Jesus teaches us that the poor in spirit understand they are human and therefore subject to mental and physical limitations. Ungodly pride, arrogance and self-absorption cause us to fall. Harsh words, hard hearts and anger trap us daily. The poor in spirit are grieved by their humanness and that awareness causes them to fall before God in misery and pain, pleading for His help and assurance.

What is the reward for being poor in spirit? The kingdom of heaven. And what is the kingdom of heaven? Peace, love, joy, faith, hope plus all that is good, noble, right and just. To be poor in spirit is to be rich with God!

Our goal then is to maintain a spirit of poorness as it keeps us in touch and dependent on God for everything. It keeps us bent in prayer, penitent and desirous of God's approval.

***Blessed are those who mourn,
for they shall be comforted.***

Picture someone mourning, crying, loud wails, rocking back and forth, falling out. Human mourning is highly visible, active and emotional. Now consider what brings on mourning. Death. Tragedy. Sin. Yes, sin. As Christians, we all have one or two "thorns", challenges, areas that we struggle with the most. For some, it's controlling the tongue, for others it's selfishness, for others it's submission. Whatever it is, this "thorn" beats us at times. If we are Christians who strive for maturity, we are immediately sorry for our failure and mourn—loudly, ugly, harshly—out of emptiness and internal pain. We also mourn because we know our failure separates us from God.

How grievous to know sin, weaknesses, a lack of discipline, transgressions, and more separate us from God. But thank God the gap exists for only a moment. For those who mourn, are grief-stricken, and truly downcast go to the Father. Broken-hearted, they fall before God contrite admitting their failures, pleading for forgiveness and repenting their ways. God, who is always good and loving and kind, hears the prayers of the penitent and rewards them. Their reward? Comfort and encouragement. A washing of His love. Reaffirmation and a peace that surpasses all understanding.

Our goal then, if we want to continue growing and maturing in Christ, is to mourn when we have fallen short and seek God's restorative blessings.

Blessed are the meek, for they shall inherit the earth.

In our society, the meek are walked-over, forced to subjection, down-trodden, as well as overlooked. To be meek in God's spiritual realm is to be highly esteemed. It is characterized by humbleness, gentleness and strength.

We are made meek by our weak human condition. We sin. We are judged. We fail to meet Jesus' standards. And yet, in spite of this, God is sure to pardon us after we have confessed our sins. We walk away from God's altar, restored and empathetic to the sins of others. We understand we are to respond to other sinners in love because we were first loved.

Our reward for meekness and humility? The earth. We walk in this present world with a smile on our face and a spring in our step. The world throws us adversity, yet it does not stick because we are spiritually equipped. Indeed, we float above all the troubles, pressures, and commands of the day because we are covered with His love and kindness. This godly condition we preserve because His Spirit controls us. Our goal then is to understand that meekness is the strength of God (power) under control.

Blessed are those who hunger and thirst for righteousness, for they shall be filled.

Have you ever felt hunger? Thirst? You know then the intensive longing for satisfaction. The painful experience of it. This is the same type of desire or longing we are to have for righteousness or right living.

When we hunger and thirst for righteousness, we crave frequent contact with God. We go to our special "date" place many times throughout the day, seeking God's wisdom and reassurance. Occasionally when the demands of the day interrupt our "filling" time with God, we feel hunger and thirst and run to re-fill ourselves with God's presence. For indeed, He is as vital and essential as water, food and air. Do you have that kind of desire for God? Do you pant, crave, long for Him? Must you have God's touch daily? Then count yourself among those who are in right-standing with God.

Your reward? You shall be filled. Not just satisfactorily filled, but an abundant filling. A filling that overwhelms and produces an outflowing of continuous thanksgiving. Our goal is to eat spiritually healthy, hearty portions of His Word many times a day.

Blessed are the merciful, for they shall obtain mercy.

All Christians know that mercy is action-oriented. We first "feel" pity and compassion but then the Holy Spirit moves us to go beyond "feeling" to "doing." The Holy Spirit prompts us to *do* something that will ease the pain and suffering of those we feel pity for. Perhaps it's dropping change in a homeless person's cup. Perhaps it is organizing a food and clothes drive for earthquake victims. Perhaps it is starting a letter-writing campaign to restore funds for social services or simply hugging a school bully and telling him he is loved. Regardless of the *doing*, mercy allows us to be the salt of the earth, that which preserves the world from utter deterioration.

Being merciful is not only directed to the unfortunate or disadvantaged it extends to those who harm, hurt or betray us. And this is the type of mercy that is harder to enact. How easy is it to love the woman who sleeps with our husband? How easy is it to follow Jesus' example of turning the other cheek when our boss humiliates us in front of our peers? How easy is it to be a Good Samaritan to one who has killed our son out of racial hate? If you cringed or gulped or side-stepped the answer to those questions, then that's a sign more spiritual maturity is needed. But don't despair; Christian maturity is a goal. It is something we strive for. So even in those times when we don't extend mercy like we ought, God still loves and remains faithful to us.

In addition to His love and faithfulness, God promises to reward us with mercy. When we make a mistake, God will grant us mercy when we have been merciful. During those times when we slip into wrong-doing, God will show mercy if we have shown mercy. God will be merciful to those who walk outside of His will, if we have been merciful. What a just and righteous God we serve!

Our goal then, if we are to grow and mature in God, is to see the offender or needy as children of God, to love them as God loves us and to act by giving them what they need.

Blessed are the pure in heart, for they shall see God.

The heart is the catch all for what we feed into our being. Do we feed it light or darkness? Do we allow sin or purity? Do we ingest the teachings of Jesus or the instructions of the world? All will know what we feed into our hearts by the things that come out of us. As scripture says, *"So a man's heart reveals the man."*

Jesus stressed to His disciples that they monitor their heart intake so that all people can tell by their actions, thoughts and deeds that they strive for a higher level of righteousness. The same instruction applies to us today. How is your heart condition? What have you allowed in?

Below are some heart questions to help you determine the content or purity of your heart.

- Do I have a pure heart that loves God first and foremost?
- Do I have an intimate fellowship with God?
- Do I surrender daily to God?
- Do I enjoy doing God's will?
- Do I mourn the "bad" in my heart?
- Am I open and honest before God and man?

- Do I serve one master...God?
- Do I act, speak and think like Jesus?

If in response to the questions, you did not "score" as high as you would have liked, there is time now to ask God to cleanse your heart. To eliminate anything in your heart that causes you to be impure or stained. He will gladly enter in and reside, swift to eliminate all things of darkness, approving only light.

For those whose hearts are pure, who "scored" well on the checklist, you are in the company of Moses. He was one whose heart was so fixed on God that his face shone from the presence of God. In this day and age, the pure in heart don't see God as Moses did but by faith, we have the opportunity to do so. God manifests His presence, His Spirit in every imaginable way. The pure in heart need only watch, wait and pray for a divine manifestation. Perhaps you will see it in a flower He blooms especially for you. Perhaps you read it in His inspired Word. Maybe it comes in the fluttering of a butterfly wing. God is ever present, always near and He makes Himself known to those who are pure in heart. This is our reward.

Our goal then to grow and mature in God, is to cleanse our heart and stay singularly focused on Him so that our face shines in His divine presence.

***Blessed are the peacemakers,
for they shall be called sons of God.***

Yahweh. Shalom. God of peace calls for his followers to be peacemakers. A peacemaker is one who seeks to glorify God by actively bringing about reconciliation and permanent peace. God is looking for His sons and daughters to uncover sin and abolish it. God is looking for His sons and daughters to eradicate hostile attitudes and search for the most equitable agreement. God wants His sons and daughters to establish and maintain peace in a dying world. Not just any son or daughter, though. It must be one who is pure in heart, poor in spirit, humble, meek, merciful, mournful and hungry for righteousness. If that is you, the field is ready to be cultivated. Every field. The field of our homes, our workplaces, our churches, our schools, our courts, etc.

New hearts, free of sin and centered on God is the end result. Peace in the fields. And most importantly, your status as a child of God. Before all the angels and hosts of heaven, God will proclaim you His own even while you are still on this earth. And on that great day, you shall receive your crown, daughter of God!

Our goal then, if we want to grow and mature in God, is to seek peace in every aspect of our life through leaning and depending on God.

Blessed are those who are persecuted for righteousness' sake, for theirs is the kingdom of heaven. Blessed are you when they revile and persecute you, and say all kinds of evil against you falsely for My sake. Rejoice and be exceedingly glad, for great is your reward in heaven, for so they persecuted the prophets who were before you.

The world does not want to be placed before a mirror to be shown all its ugliness. Yet, that is what true followers of Jesus do just as Jesus did in His time. True believers promote the values and character of Jesus. That places us in a position to be persecuted. We will have accusations hurled at us, be lied about and ridiculed, be mocked and misunderstood and yet, we continue advancing God's kingdom here on earth supported by the knowledge that persecution is a blessing.

A blessing? Yes. Our reward for subjecting ourselves to persecution just as the prophets before us. We are blessed because we have been judged to be in His image and likeness. We are blessed because God's will is ours. We rejoice and are glad and welcome the undeserved and unfair treatment.

God sees how we are unjustly treated in our homes, workplaces, churches, schools, social arenas and opens the doors of heaven to pour out an overflowing blessing. God also rewards by placing a pleasing mark by our name in the Book of Life.

Persecution is our barometer for determining if we are Christlike in our daily interactions and living.

"You are the salt of the earth; but if the salt loses its flavor, how shall it be seasoned? It is then good for nothing but to be thrown out and trampled underfoot by men." From this seemingly simple statement of Jesus, as *salty* women of God, we understand:

Salt is distinctively different from the object in which it is put on. As godly women, we are to be distinctively different. We are called to be the salt of the earth. *We are not to be conformed to this world, but we are to be transformed by the renewing of our minds.* We must be different from the

world and everything the world stands for.
Salt preserves and keeps things from spoiling or going bad.

Salt cleanses. Like salt, we believers are to help cleanse and preserve the world from corruption and decay.

Salt penetrates. It changes the thing that it is put on. Godly women, we must penetrate the world and help change things for the better.

Salt flavors. Anytime salt is applied, it influences the taste of a thing. It takes a tasteless piece of food and adds flavor. Can you imagine eating an egg white without salt? We are to influence and flavor this world for Christ.

Salt is quiet. It works without being seen. It does its work quietly.

Salt spreads. We must sprinkle salt throughout the world.

Salt is irrepressible. Once salt is applied, it cannot be stopped. Our testimony is irrepressible. It must not be stopped.

The world, in its deteriorating state, is waiting for someone to come and spread a little seasoning. Could that someone be you? Yes, woman of God, it is you!

Remember, you are a loved and blessed child of God! And He is with you all the way!

Points to Ponder:

➢ When we give God our weaknesses, He gives us sufficiency, causing us to do exceedingly great things.

➢ The mature believer understands their growth in God is achieved through the daily, multiple decisions they make. Either you decide for God or against God.

➢ The Beatitudes presuppose Jesus Christ as our personal Savior and assumes the Holy Spirit dwells within us. Hence, non-believers stand outside the Beatitudes, lost and confused, until they confess Jesus Christ as Lord and Savior.

➢ Changing into a mature believer is not possible within our own power. We must rely on the strength of God. Cry out! He will be quick to respond.

Questions to Consider:

1. Are the intangible blessings God offers enough to make us want to achieve a higher level of godliness?

   _____

   _____

2. Has God convicted you of a certain stronghold or "thorn"?

   _____

   _____

3. What have you done to achieve victory over that thing?

   _____

   _____

4. What specific action helps you through the struggle?

   _____

   _____

5. Tell of a personal experience where you reaped what you sowed.

   _____
   _____

A Woman
and
Her Body

The Challenge to Change

As a woman of God you are to be stately and strong like the powerful pillars that support magnificent mansions. Your head should be up, mind sharp, body in excellent condition, and spirit soaring high because you know who you are in God and know the purpose for which He has created you. Additionally, we want to look and feel our very best. Accomplishing this is not always easy given our busy, complex lives and countless responsibilities. However, priority must be given to developing the total you if you are to fulfill the purpose and plan God has for you. God wants us to be focused on maintaining our bodies and to experience the joy of balance in all aspects of our lives.

As you can see, folding the physical in with the spiritual, emotional and mental aspects of our lives is of significant importance and you possess two major tools to help you reach these goals--your mind and your body. Both must be maintained with the utmost care. Just like it is easier and more cost effective to maintain a mansion than it is to repair it, the same is true of the human body. We therefore commit, as godly women, to maintain a life of good health, strong minds, balanced emotions and nutrition wellness.

Knowledge and the appropriate actions can counteract these facts and statistics; hence, we take time now to learn how health, nutrition and wellness checks (preventive maintenance) can positively defeat these facts and improve our body image and self-confidence. Did you know your health and nutrition affect your body image? Did you know health and nutrition affect how you feel as well as how you look? Did you know self-confidence can be linked to health and nutrition? Good! Then you also know your body weight is derived from how you eat, the nutrients you consume or don't consume, your lifestyle and your daily decisions. Given this, we strive for "healthy weight."

Healthy weight is not determined by a generic height/weight chart in your doctor's office, but by the weight at which you can live a comfortable, reasonable life. It is the weight at which your unique body settles when you are not overindulging in foods and obsessing about diet and exercise. Indeed, this is what we refer to as your "ideal" weight. In maintaining a healthy body weight, we discover it is not about weight at all, but rather the decisions we make on a day-to-day basis to meet our health and nutritional needs.

How many times a day do we reach for a candy bar? How many meals do we drink from a can? How many meals a day do we eat from fast-food restaurants? Yes, it is often more convenient and easier to do these things, but these habits and decisions do not provide us with the nutrition we need to be healthy and fit. We cannot make unhealthy decisions and expect to stay at or achieve our healthy or ideal weight.

Consider your daily eating habits. Now, compare it to the recommended daily dietary needs of most women. Your daily diet should contain a wide variety of foods such as vegetables, fruits, and grains. It should also include low-fat dairy products, lean meats, poultry, fish and legumes.

We should strive to decrease the amount of sugar, salt, and saturated fats that we intake. We should also remember to drink plenty of water. By eating a wholesome diet, well stocked with all the daily nutrients, minerals and vitamins needed, we give our bodies the fuel it needs to function properly. We also reduce the risk of osteoporosis (bone loss), anemia (iron deficiency) and other conditions and diseases. There's no doubt health and nutrition are important elements in attaining a fit body. Another element we cannot ignore if we are to maintain our stately temples is preventive medical check-ups. Screening tests, preventive medicine and immunizations assist in keeping our bodies fit for God's purpose.

Regardless of the risk level, all women should have the following tests:

- Mammograms
- Pap Smears
- Cholesterol Checks
- Blood Pressure
- Colorectal Cancer Tests
- Diabetes Tests
- Osteoporosis Tests

It is highly recommended that every woman consult with her doctor to determine what tests are right for her, how often the tests should be administered and (age) the tests should be scheduled. As stated earlier, it is much better to maintain your body than to repair it. And these tests, immunizations and the medicines your doctor may have already prescribed are sure ways to keep your body fit and able to do God's will.

The above information provides knowledge and knowledge is what propels us to improve our nutrition choices, to stay abreast of our medical check-ups and to change our previous mindset. But, as we know by now, change is never easy. Many of us will make several attempts to change our daily decisions and lifestyle before successfully reaching our goal. The reason for this is temptation. Every day, several times a day, we will be tempted to stay in the old eating or lifestyle rut, but do not give in to the old way or become discouraged. Seek God in prayer and stay in His Word and He will provide a way to overcome your temptation.

An excellent way to stay on track with your commitment to better health, nutrition and wellness is to set a plan of action. Your plan for achieving and maintaining good health should include:

- Set Realistic goals.
- Gradually phase out old habits.
- Surround yourself with supportive individuals.
- Communicate openly your thoughts, feelings, and needs. Understand why you're eating when you're not hungry, why you eat dessert when you're already full, why you're afraid to eat certain foods.
- Foresee difficult situations and avoid them.
- Read God's Word.

- Keep your eyes on the prize that comes with reaching your goal.

A plan of action is a solid defense against temptation especially if the plan is written and referred to as often as necessary. Should you slip one day into your old rut, acknowledge your mistake, then pick up where you left off. It is also rewarding to meditate on the fact that God is on your side and will provide encouragement as you go through this process of enhancing your godly temple.

Points to Ponder:

- ➤ God wants me to be well emotionally, spiritually, mentally, and physically.
- ➤ My body is the temple of God and I must take care of it.
- ➤ One of the best ways to overcome temptation is to rely on God's word.
- ➤ God has a plan for my life and I must be healthy in order to carry it out effectively.

Questions to Consider:

1. What are some of the things that hinder me from achieving my health, nutrition and wellness goals?

   _____

   _____

2. What foods do I indulge in that I know are bad for my health?

   _____

   _____

3. What positive steps can I make right now that will put me on track to achieving a healthier lifestyle?

   _____

   _____

4. Who in my life will be a great supporter as I change to a healthier diet?

   _____

   _____

Self-Esteem Matters

Are you happy with who you are? What you look like? If you answered yes, you are one who has mastered the definition of 'real beauty.' A woman of real beauty is one who has a positive self-image, who is comfortable with who she is, secure in her womanhood, and most importantly has an "inner glow."

Inner glow is not birthed from the make-up you apply, the color of your hair or the beautiful clothes that drape your body. Inner glow is born from loving yourself, taking care of yourself and affirming and honoring yourself. In other words, a woman of real beauty has healthy self-esteem and knowledge of her identity in Christ, something no amount of make-up can provide.

Woman of God, you are beautiful, but if you need help believing that, if you need help uncovering your inner beauty, I recommend the following:

- *Exercise regularly.*

- *Eat well.* Include lots of fruits and vegetables and plenty of water in your diet.

- *Get plenty of rest.* You feel better when you're getting enough sleep.

- *Focus on the things you like about yourself.* If you've got great eyes, play them up! Beautiful hands? Keep them well-manicured.

- *Develop your interests and hobbies.* If you've always wanted to paint, take an art class. If you're a good dancer, take dance lessons.

- *Take time to pursue your purpose.* Take a step every day towards your goal. For example, if your goal is to be a writer, write down the steps it will take for you to accomplish that goal:

  1. Schedule time to write and stick to it.
  2. Take a writing class to brush up on writing skills.
  3. Subscribe to newsletters and/or journals that encourage and motivate you.
  4. Talk with experts, listen to their advice, etc.
  5. Show others your work!

- *Take time for others.* Nothing makes us feel better than lending a helping hand to someone in need. Be a Big Sister or volunteer your time to help someone in need.

- *Keep a journal.* Write down your daily thoughts and feelings. Journaling will help you to learn more about yourself as you keep track of the things that are going on in your life.

- *Listen to your body.* Each of us has a different internal "schedule." Pay attention to yours. Eat when you're hungry, sleep when you're tired, etc.

- *Smile.* People tend to be attracted to those who are happy.

- *Commune with God.* Writing, talking, singing, playing music, and meditating are all ways in which you can communicate with God.

- *Study God's Word.* Consider the following as you read, study and meditate on Biblical scriptures:

    1. Use a daily devotional as a reading guide.
    2. Follow a systematic plan for reading through the Bible.
    3. Get involved in a Bible Study group.
    4. Use a Bible that contains study notes and references.

- *Use a prayer list.* Write down the things you are praying for such as important issues in your life and in the lives of those you know, world issues, governmental leaders, church leaders, etc. Keeping track of answered prayers will encourage you to continue praying.

While it is important for us to be aware of our external appearance, to look good and feel good, we must couple that with God's knowledge. In His Word, King David says, *"I will praise You, for I am fearfully and wonderfully made; Marvelous are Your works, and that my soul knows very well."* Like King David, we should praise God for we are indeed wonderfully formed by His hands.

Knowing and believing this, we incorporate faith and prayer into our health, nutrition and beauty regime. This allows us to develop our inner beauty—the real beauty—and to celebrate the miracle that is us, God's creation. In fact, make it a point to take time every day to incorporate God and His Word into your daily beauty regime and to celebrate you. As talk show host Oprah Winfrey once said, "The more you praise and celebrate your life, the more there is in life to celebrate."

Self-esteem is another characteristic we should all strive for in our goal of obtaining real beauty. What is self-esteem? In *The Anxiety and Phobia Workbook*, Dr. Edmund J. Bourne defines self-esteem as, "a way of thinking, feeling, and acting that implies that you accept, respect, trust, and believe in yourself." Some other words that describe self-esteem include confidence, satisfaction, and love.

As women of God, we should shun any definition of self-esteem that suggests our value depends on any external condition. Our self-esteem is never based on the impression or reaction of others or what is going right or wrong in our lives. Instead, we operate in a frame of mind that always convey our identity in God. We believe in ourselves, we value ourselves, we accept our uniqueness and importance, and we celebrate our lives because we understand we are God's miracle.

The women of God who think in these terms possess high self-esteem. They think of themselves in a positive light and feel confident that they are able to make positive changes in their lives. They tend to be productive, flexible, and competent. They do not have emotional or behavioral issues but enjoy personal and professional lives that are balanced, open, honest, and assertive. In short, women with high self-esteem love themselves, take care of themselves, and treat others with love, thoughtfulness, and respect.

Unfortunately, this is not the case for all women of God. There are some who suffer from low self-esteem. They often think of themselves in a negative manner and make negative comments about themselves. They tend to be anxious, depressed, bitter, and angry. They also tend to be ineffective, unprofessional, and incompetent in their personal and professional lives. Below are some behaviors, feelings or thoughts that characterize women of low self-esteem.

- Think poorly of themselves and consider themselves unworthy
- Often select unrealistic goals or shy away from challenges
- Tend to be pessimistic about the future
- Operate out of a fear of rejection

- Are typically unassertive in their interactions with others

- Are fearful of conflict with others

- Respond negatively to criticism or other kinds of negative feedback

- Crave the approval of others

- Find it difficult to accept compliments or recognition from others

Who Do You Say You Are?

Who am I? Who do I belong to? What is my family lineage? These are seemingly easy questions to answer. Did you respond in the spiritual or the flesh? Did you answer at the surface or complex level? Did you respond honestly or avoid answering all together? How you answered tells a lot about the thoughts in your head and the feelings in your heart.

Hold on to those questions and your responses for in this lesson we continue our study of self-esteem, seeking to understand who we really are and how to combat that which we are not. We start with where we originally started—God.

"Who do you say that I am?" This question Jesus posed to his disciples after performing a series of miracles. After reciting a list of titles, one disciple finally answers, *"You are the Christ."* From Jesus' acceptance of the disciple's answer, we take our cue on how to answer the questions above. We are believers and followers of Christ. It's just that simple. We belong to Christ, we are in the

family of Christ and we share the blood of Christ. Therefore, as believers and followers of Jesus Christ, we believe wholeheartedly Ephesians 2:10 which tells us, "...*we are His workmanship, created in Christ Jesus for good works...*" and later in Ephesians 4, verse 24, "*...put on the new man which was created according to God, in true righteousness and holiness.*"

Remembering these truths and instilling them in our hearts and minds forces us to turn loose anything that separates us from God and that includes low self-esteem. Yes, we sometimes revisit that condition because so many of us are negatively impacted by it.

One of the symptoms of poor self-esteem is that one constantly re-defines themselves. A woman with low self-esteem will sway and blow with the wind, latching on to fads, trends and new images as fast as the media throws them at us. She is not deeply rooted in Christ and therefore steps outside her ministry, her purpose, her mission easily. That's not beneficial to her or God. That's why it is so critical that the woman with low self-esteem come to terms with who she is in God and that she commits to a healthy self-image.

It is challenging—but not impossible—to recover from low self-esteem. A strong relationship with an identity in God is the first step of recovery, but in severe cases where a woman's self-esteem has reached the profoundly impacted level, that is not enough. In these cases, individual counseling is an option. A counselor or therapist will help you deal with any irrational thinking, distorted feelings, and destructive behaviors that promote low self-esteem. Group counseling is another option for recovery. These counseling sessions allow victims of low self-esteem to work together on self-confidence, anger or control issues in a setting where honest feedback and confrontation are tools used to build self-worth.

A short-term, inpatient stay at a hospital or clinic may be a third option for the profoundly impacted woman. During a hospital or clinic stay, the patient will be guided through a recovery program, such as the Self-Esteem Seekers Anonymous' 12-step program. This program is designed to help women dig to the root of self-esteem issues by confronting self-destructive behaviors, self-defeating patterns, and irrational thinking.

In addition to the options mentioned above, a woman battling low self-esteem may want to journal. In her journal, she may want to address the following and record her accomplishments and improvements.

- Confront the distorted thoughts, feelings, and behaviors stemming from the sources of low self-esteem.

- Dispel any irrational beliefs and seek to learn what is normal. Get in touch with reality.

- Replace negative self-scripts with daily self-affirmations.

- Identify and label all feelings, both negative and positive.

- Practice expressing feelings, needs, and wants in a direct, honest manner and reinforce feelings of being a valuable person worthy to be listened to.

- Make sure wants, needs and feelings are considered by others.

- Develop an intimate relationship with God; open up to Him; trust God with your feelings; let Him heal you!

- Identify self-defeating behaviors and change them.

- Change unhealthy behaviors by acting only on rational thoughts and true feelings.

- Accept personal responsibility for the quality of your life; accept personal responsibility for your actions and no longer blame others.

- Learn to leave the past in the past and abandon your old past or identity. Do not allow one event or multiple events from the past determine your now.

- Treat mistakes as opportunities for learning.

- Set short and long-term goals that will demonstrate growth in self-esteem in both your personal and professional life.

- Give to God the issues you cannot control or change in your life and allow Him to handle them.

- Know what the Word of God says about you. Read and reflect on the following scriptures:
    - Ephesians 2:10
    - Romans 5:6-8
    - Romans 15:7
    - Matthew 5:48
    - Colossians 3:13
    - John 15:14-15
    - Psalm 139:13-14
    - Isaiah 43:7, 10, 21
    - Matthew 25:40
    - Psalm 145:14
    - Ephesians 3:17-19

Learn to live on purpose by focusing on the unique gifts given to you by God and the specific purpose for which He created you.

For further assistance in recovering from low self-esteem, Dr. Edmund J. Bourne, in *The Anxiety and Phobia Workbook*, offers the Personal Bill of Rights. These principles, written below, should be recited every day until they are ingrained in actions, feelings and thoughts.

Personal Bill of Rights

- I have the right to ask for what I want.
- I have the right to say no to requests or demands I can't meet.
- I have the right to express all of my feelings, positive or negative.

- I have the right to change my mind.
- I have the right to make mistakes and not have to be perfect.
- I have the right to follow my own values and standards.
- I have the right to say no to anything when I feel I am not ready, it is unsafe, or it violates my values.
- I have the right to determine my own priorities.
- I have the right not to be responsible for others' behavior, actions, feelings, or problems.
- I have the right to expect honesty from others.
- I have the right to be angry at someone I love.
- I have the right to be uniquely myself.
- I have the right to feel scared and say, "I'm afraid."
- I have the right to say, "I don't know."
- I have the right not to give excuses or reasons for my behavior.
- I have the right to make decisions based on my feelings.
- I have the right to my own need for personal space and time.
- I have the right to be playful and frivolous.
- I have the right to be healthier than those around me.
- I have the right to be in a non-abusive environment.

- I have the right to make friends and be comfortable around people.
- I have the right to change and grow.
- I have the right to have my needs and wants respected by others.
- I have the right to be treated with dignity and respect.
- I have the right to be happy.

Remember, moving from low self-esteem to high self-esteem requires a change in thought, feelings and behavior. As we've learned from other areas that require change, change takes time and setbacks and relapses often occur. Don't beat yourself up when immediate or moderate improvement isn't recognized. Acknowledge the failure, analyze the misstep, reset yourself and start again. Keep fighting to be the child of God you are supposed to be. There is no one but you keeping you from it!

Points to Ponder:

- I am beautiful on the inside; hence, I am beautiful on the outside.
- No amount of make-up can make me beautiful if I do not possess inner beauty.
- Faith and prayer are essential to real beauty.
- Talking to God and studying His Word will help me see myself as the beautiful person He created me to be.
- I am a valuable human being, worthy to love and be loved.
- I am responsible for developing my own sense of value and self-worth.
- I will love myself unconditionally.
- Only I can define who I am. No one else, other than God, has the right to do so.
- No one event or multiple events can define who I am.
- I will confront any distorted thoughts, feelings, and behaviors I have about myself.
- I will treat the mistakes I make in my life as opportunities to learn and grow.
- No one except me can keep me from reaching my goal of high self-esteem.

Questions to Consider:

1. Do I allow the media to set my standards of beauty?

   _____
   _____

2. Do I focus more on my outward beauty than my inner beauty?

   _____
   _____

3. What can I do to ensure that I am beautiful on the inside?

   _____
   _____

4. Am I dealing inwardly with any self-esteem issues? If so, what are they?

   _____
   _____

5. Do I have any problems in my personal or professional life that may stem from feelings of low self-worth?

_____

_____

6. How can God and His Word help me value myself more?

_____

_____

7. What can I say to encourage someone dealing with low self-esteem to seek counseling?

_____

_____

8. What steps can I take to ensure that I am responsible for my own actions?

_____

_____

Understanding Who You Are

As children of God, we know that we are created in His image. We've read in the Bible that we are not only God's children, but "joint heirs" with Christ. We've even read where our beloved Savior said that if we believe on Him, we can do greater works than He did while here on earth. But do we really believe these things to be true? Do we really believe that we are miracles, uniquely created with divineness in us?

If we really believed in the miracle of our lives, we would not ignore our miraculous bodies or allow it to be defiled. If we really believed ourselves to be miracles, we would not degrade ourselves nor allow others to abuse us. If we really believed in the miracle of being alive, we would live every day on purpose, striving to fulfill God's will for our lives.

Your challenge today is to accept the miraculousness that surrounds your life. You must acknowledge the fact that you are part of a greater plan, that you were created with purpose and destiny within you. You must truly believe that you - with all of your shortcomings, failures, disappointments, and problems - are the world's greatest miracle. Only then will you be able to confront your fears and change your life forever. Only then will you be able to develop and implement strategies to regain control of the emotional, mental, physical and spiritual aspects of your life. Only then will you be able to celebrate the valuable person that you are.

When you begin to celebrate the miracle of your life and use your God-given right and responsibility to take care of yourself, you will begin to affect those around you and they will be compelled to share in this divine, miraculous experience. Marianne Williamson summed it up best in her book A Return to Love: Reflections of the Principles of a Course in Miracles recited by Nelson Mandela in his inaugural address:

> *"Our deepest fear is not that we are inadequate.*
> *Our deepest fear is that we are powerful beyond measure.*
> *It's our light, not our darkness that most frightens us.*
> *We ask ourselves, who am I to be*
> *brilliant, gorgeous, talented, and fabulous?*
> *Actually, who are you not to be?*
> *You are a child of God.*
> *Playing small doesn't serve the world.*
> *There's nothing enlightened about shrinking*
> *so that other people won't feel insecure around you.*
> *We were born to make manifest the glory of God that is within us. It's not just in some of us; it's in everyone.*
> *And as we let our light shine, we unconsciously give other people permission to do the same.*
> *As we are liberated from our own fear,*
> *our presence automatically liberates others."*

Points to Ponder:

- I am the world's greatest miracle.
- When I face my fears, I can change my life for the better... forever.
- Minimizing my gifts and talents do not serve the world or the purpose for which God created me.
- Because I was created in God's image, I am powerful beyond measure.

Questions to Consider:

1. Do I really believe I am a miracle? If not, what stops me from believing so?

   _____
   _____

2. What one thing can I do daily to celebrate the miracle of my life?

   _____
   _____

3. How can I allow the light within me to shine through so that others can see the miraculous things God has done in me?

   _____
   _____

Message From The Author

My Dear Ladies,

I pray that by now, you have begun to live your lives on purpose and walk in your unique calling. Ask God to renew your minds and be who you were created to be. I encourage you to **Value You!** Celebrate You! Pursue your purpose and live it out every minute of every day. After all, it is your life, live it on purpose.

It is my desire that this book will become an "heirloom" that is passed down through many, generations to encourage women of all ages, to walk in their God given purpose. Use this book for your personal time and group Bible studies.

Be Blessed!

Mother Ida Hathman

Acknowledgements

The Bible tells us that a man who finds a wife finds a good thing; however, every day I reverse that scripture and thank God that I had a "good-thing" man in my life...my husband, the late Willie Hathman. Willie knew I was capable even when I doubted. His support through fifty years of marriage was unfailing.

Children are a blessing and Willie and I experienced that blessing many times. To all my children: My son Eric and all my daughters Paula, Adra, Juwana, Matra, Regina and Crystal, I pass to you my heartfelt thanks for coloring my life with love, for allowing me to gain wisdom through motherhood and for the life experiences that became (and continue to become) the foundation for S. A. L. T. (Save A Life Today Ministries)

To my church family, Ambassadors Today, I say Thank You for all your prayers, kind words, and encouragement. You hold a special place in my heart.

To all my SALT Girls, wherever you are, I LOVE YOU! You made this possible! Remember I see you and you have made me proud!

And finally, to my Pastor and daughter Dr. Regina Spellmon, who taught and is still teaching me the Word of God and who labors with me in the ministry, I offer a very special God bless and thanks!

May God continue to abundantly bless every facet of your lives! I love you all!

About the Author

Ida Brown Hathman, also called Mom or Mother Hathman, is a wife, mother, grandmother, great-grand mother, sister... and "unofficial" mother to many.

She was born in Tennessee Colony, Texas on a farm and upon graduation from high school moved to Chicago to continue her education. Later, she returned to Texas, settling in Fort Worth, where she met and married Willie Hathman, Jr. After a lengthy career with the United States Postal Service, Mrs. Hathman resigned her position and continued to pursue her goal as an entrepreneur. In 1984, she opened a hair and nail salon. It was then, while operating this salon, that the concept for Save A Life Today Ministries was birthed and formed while holding the hands of many women and listening to them as they painfully poured out their broken hearts. S. A. L. T. is a vehicle that God has ordained to help change many lives through this woman of God.

In Christian service and duty, Mrs. Hathman is an ordained Minister of the Gospel and Director of The Women's Department at Ambassadors Today where Dr. Regina Spellmon is Senior Pastor. In line with her other talents, gifts and skills, Mrs. Hathman has the spirit of an apostle, one who catches the spirit and makes new visions come to pass. She has also served as Sunday School teacher, Church Administrator, School Administrator (Ambassadors of Christ Christian Academy) and Minister of Education. Mrs. Hathman is credited for her completed studies in both institutions of higher learning and accredited Bible Colleges where she earned her Master of Minister Degree.

Mrs. Hathman is not only the founder of Save A Life Today Ministries, Inc., but also an esteemed woman of God. This is not a surprise to anyone who knows her first name, Ida, means Godly. Mrs. Hathman has incorporated her name into her personal mission which is to "touch as many lives as she can and add flavor or seasoning to enhance the lives of women." She strives to leave an imprint on the lives of everyone she encounters and for future generations to come.

SEASONED SALT

www.ingramcontent.com/pod-product-compliance
Lightning Source LLC
Chambersburg PA
CBHW071855070526
44583CB00016B/1706